The Sea Power Library

DESTROYERS

The Sea Power Library

DESTROYERS

by Max Walmer

Rourke Publications, Inc.
Vero Beach, Florida 32964

Lean and mean, fitted out for a fight at speed, destroyers are among the most glamorous warships in the U.S. Navy.

Library of Congress Cataloging-in-Publication Data
Walmer, Max.
  Destroyers
  (The Sea power library)
  Includes index.
  Summary: Describes the history, types, weapons, and present uses of destroyers, both in the United States and the Soviet Union.
  1. Destroyers (Warships) — Juvenile literature.
[1. Destroyers (Warships)] I. Title. II. Series.
V825.W35   1989   359.3'254   88-30697
ISBN 0-86625-081-6

Contents

Modern Destroyers

A low-angle aerial shot of the port bow of the USS F. T. Berry.

Destroyers have long been the most glamorous and dashing of warships. They are lean and mean fighting machines, heavily armed for their size, fast, highly maneuverable and traditionally always in the thick of the battle.

The name "destroyer" is actually a shortened form of the original name, which was "torpedo-boat destroyer." This type of ship originated in the 1890s when the battle fleets of the day — large, lumbering battleships with a flank speed of no more than 15 **knots** — found themselves threatened by crafts that were light, fast, and agile. These ships, of around 100 tons **displacement**, were armed with torpedoes. It became necessary to do something about these "torpedo-boats"; the answer was the "torpedo-boat destroyer." The first such boats were designed quite simply by doubling the size and displacement of the torpedo boats they were intended to destroy. They displaced some 240 tons, carried a 12-pound gun, three 6-pounders, and one 18-inch torpedo tube. They were powered by reciprocating engines, which gave them a speed of 26 knots, very fast for that time. They were, in fact, so successful that within ten years they had totally replaced the torpedo-boats they had been designed to combat.

All navies found that destroyers were capable of undertaking many tasks, such as scouting, escorting larger warships and merchantmen, and independent missions. Destroyers in groups could even attack battleships. Their high speed and good maneuverability, combined with the use of smokescreens, made them exceptionally difficult to

An aerial port-quarter bow view of the destroyer USS George F. Davis under way in the Indian Ocean.

deal with. The more adventurous officers and seamen of all navies enjoyed serving on destroyers. Despite the discomfort and crowded conditions, they were exciting, and the discipline was much more lax than on the big battleships and cruisers.

By World War One (1914 — 1918) destroyers were four times the size of the original torpedo-boat destroyer, displacing over 1,000 tons. They were powered by oil-fired steam turbines, giving them a speed of about 35 to 36 knots — almost the same speed as today's destroyers. The main weapons, however, were still 3-inch guns and 21-inch torpedoes. In the early part of the war destroyers were used primarily with the battle fleets, warding off enemy destroyers or carrying out torpedo attacks on the enemy battle fleet. But, World War One also saw the appearance of the submarine as a major weapon, and German U-boats wrought havoc on British and American merchant ships taking supplies to Western Europe across the Atlantic. It quickly became obvious that the destroyer was the ideal type of warship to hunt and kill these new menaces under the surface of the ocean.

From the deck of the USS **Kidd**, *the huge Kuwaiti tanker* **Bridgeton** *is shown under way en route to open waters.*

Assigned to Military Sealift Command, this diesel-powered navy cargo ship is one of several military vessels that destroyers would protect in time of war.

The USS Henry B. Wilson, a typical Adams-class destroyer, has a displacement of 4,500 tons and carries a combined crew of 360 officers and men.

Between the two world wars, destroyers continued to grow in size and capability. More guns and torpedo tubes were mounted and new devices, such as **sonar** to detect submarines, were fitted. In World War Two destroyers were used extensively to attack both enemy submarines and enemy surface ships. The air threats in the Mediterranean and the Pacific, however, meant that anti-aircraft defense became an additional and highly important role. The ultimate wartime development of the American destroyer,

The U.S. Navy presently operates 31 Spruance-class destroyers, each of which displaces more than 7,800 tons fully loaded.

incorporating the lessons of four hard-fought years of war against the Japanese, is represented by the Gearing class. These ships displaced 3,749 tons and their primary weapons systems were four 5-inch dual-purpose (**DP**) guns and six 3-inch anti-aircraft (**AA**) guns, all radar-controlled, together with a number of visually controlled 40mm Bofors AA guns. For anti-submarine warfare (**ASW**) there were six 18-inch torpedo tubes, a Hedgehog depth-bomb launcher and depth charges. Geared steam turbines delivered 60,000 horsepower, driving the ship at a flank speed of 35 knots.

After 1945, the huge number of war-built destroyers satisfied most navies' needs for many years. When post-war ship construction started, destroyers' size again increased rapidly to accommodate the new weapons and sensors navies wanted to put on them. The Gearing class had a displacement of 3,749 tons, for example, but the Forrest Sherman class, constructed in the 1950s, displaced 4,200 tons, while the 1960s Coontz class displaced no less than 6,150 tons.

Built between 1962 and 1964, the Adams-class destroyer USS Benjamin Stoddert *shows off its clean lines.*

The starboard bow view of the guided-missile destroyer USS Kidd under way during operations in the Persian Gulf.

The largest destroyers operated by the U.S. Navy are the four Kidd-class, represented here by the flagship.

A major influence beginning in the 1950s was the rapid spread of missile systems. Missiles themselves are relatively light, but their magazines and handling rooms take up a considerable amount of internal volume. Anti-aircraft missiles require large radar scanners mounted as high as possible, which adds to the top weight.

The appearance of nuclear submarines also posed new challenges for surface ASW ships. Nuclear-powered submarines were much faster than diesel-electric submarines and could maintain these high speeds almost indefinitely. For example, the fastest diesel-electric submarine of 1960 could travel underwater at 20 knots for about one hour, whereas the nuclear-powered **USS** *Skate* could travel at about 30 knots almost indefinitely. These new submarines posed a significant threat to carrier groups and convoys. Destroyers now not only had to be more effective in the air-defense (**AD**) role but in the ASW role as well. Better sensors were needed, together with more capable weapons systems. Despite the displacement of destroyers increasing to about 6,000 tons, it became necessary to introduce a degree of role specialization.

Kidd-class destroyers are the same size as small cruisers of the Belknap class, represented here by the USS Wainwright.

Weapons Systems

Modern destroyers are armed with guns, missiles, torpedoes, and close-in weapons systems (**CIWS**), the actual balance of the mix depending upon the primary mission of the ship. Further, since no modern weapon can be utilized on its own, destroyers have to be fitted with numerous sensors to find and identify the targets and to control the missiles or guns used to attack them. At one stage in the 1960s, advocates of missile armament became so powerful that ships were built without any guns at all, relying instead upon missiles alone. This proved to be an error, and all navies now build destroyers with a balance of guns and missiles. The gun still has many roles, in shore bombardment, in carrying out limited engagements against other ships, and against incoming missiles and aircraft.

Represented here by the USS Merrill, *Spruance-class destroyers are built on the modular concept, whereby major sections of the ship are designed to fit other separately built modules.*

Today's U.S. destroyer gun is the 127mm Mark 45 DP gun, which can be used against surface or airborne targets. It is automatic, firing 16 to 20 rounds per minute; there are no men in the turret, but six are required below decks to reload the ammunition drums. The gun has a range against surface targets of 25,900 yards and a ceiling against airborne targets of 48,700 feet.

Missiles are the primary form of defense against sea and air targets.

A major threat to modern warships comes from low-flying enemy aircraft and sea-skimming missiles. It is best to counter these by destroying them as far away as possible, but they are difficult to detect either visually or by radar because they fly so low. Therefore the destroyer needs close-in weapons systems (**CIWS**) to provide "last-ditch" defense. These systems need to have extremely short response times and such a high rate of fire that they effectively erect a curtain of steel between the ship and the missile. The U.S. Navy's answer to this problem is the very successful Mark 15 Vulcan-Phalanx system, in which a 20mm six-barreled gatling gun is

incorporated into an intelligent, fully automatic, closed-loop control system. In this control system the incoming missile and the outgoing projectiles are tracked by radar and the system uses the angular error between the two to correct the point of aim of the next burst. Maximum range is 1,500 yards, but accuracy increases as the missile approaches, peaking at 550 yards. Ammunition rounds are made from **depleted uranium**, and 1,000 are housed in a magazine below the fire unit. Most ships in the U.S. fleet now mount Phalanx, and the system is also used by many foreign navies.

From Harpoon missile launchers to small arms, U.S. Navy destroyers carry a complete range of weapons against all sea and air threats.

Harpoon is a high-speed anti-ship tactical cruise missile, operational with many U.S. Navy destroyers.

The latest U.S. Navy destroyers are equipped with the Standard surface-to-air missile for defense against aircraft.

Harpoon has a range of more than 50 miles and carries a high-explosive penetrating warhead.

One mission assigned to most destroyers is that of anti-submarine warfare. The standard ship-borne ASW weapon on U.S. destroyers is the Mark 46 torpedo. This is launched from the main deck, and the torpedo runs out automatically until it is well clear of its own ship before going into a spiral search pattern to detect the enemy submarine. It is fitted with an "active/passive" homing head, which means that it begins its search for the enemy submarine using the passive mode to home in on the target's radiated noise (for example, from the noise created by its propeller turning). Passive homing has the advantage that the submarine cannot detect the incoming torpedo, but if this fails then the torpedo automatically switches on its active sonar detector, which can sense even a stationary submarine operating on a "quiet routine."

The Mark 46 torpedo is 102 inches long and 12.75 inches in diameter. Its warhead contains no less than 100 pounds of high explosive. The torpedo is driven by a liquid-fuel motor, and twin, contra-rotating propellers give it a speed of 45 knots and a range of 12,000 yards at a depth of 50 feet.

The anti-submarine rocket (**ASROC**) enables ASW ships to attack hostile submarines at some distance from the ship. The ASROC missile consists of two sections. The propulsion section is a solid-propellant rocket motor, whose burn time is regulated to achieve the desired range. The warhead can be either a nuclear depth bomb with a yield of approximately 1 **kiloton** (1KT), or a Mark 46 anti-submarine torpedo. The torpedo-equipped version of ASROC is 16.7 feet long and weighs about 1,653 pounds; its range is approximately 1.25 to 6.2 miles.

Until the 1980s the standard ASROC launcher was a box-shaped, 8-cell device, capable of being trained in arc and elevation, and mounted on destroyers' upper decks. The new Arleigh Burke class, however, will be fitted with vertical launch tubes mounted under the foredeck. On launch ASROC follows a ballistic trajectory until it reaches a point which has been predetermined by the launch control computer, where the rocket motor is jettisoned. If the payload is a torpedo, it then descends by parachute to the sea's surface, where its motor is activated and its homing head switches on and starts to search for the enemy submarine. If the warhead is a nuclear depth bomb, it free-falls into the sea and descends to a predetermined depth, where it is detonated by a pressure-sensitive fuse.

In combat, destroyers operate in association with cruisers like this Ticonderoga-class vessel, seen here launching an anti-aircraft missile.

Modern ship missiles are carried in special box launchers linked to radar units that seek out and track enemy targets.

Ship-launched missiles are guided to their targets by radar or special sensors that seek out the target.

In the Persian Gulf, a gunner aboard the USS Fox *mans a 50-caliber machine gun.*

The principal ASW weapons system of a modern U.S. destroyer is its helicopter. Older ships carry the **LAMPS-**I helicopter, the Kaman SH-2F Seasprite. This excellent aircraft has given many years' service, but it is now being replaced by the larger, more modern, and much more capable LAMPS-III helicopter, the Sikorsky SH-60B Seahawk. The SH-60B takes off and lands on a helicopter platform usually mounted near the stern of the destroyer. During its flight, it is in constant communication with its parent ship, using radio to pass both commands and data. On an ASW mission the helicopter flies to its search area and then drops a pattern of **sonobuoys**, which float in the water and use sonar detectors to search for enemy submarines. The sonobuoys pass data by a radio-link to the helicopter, which relays it back to the destroyer, where the information is used on the ASW plot. The helicopter also has a powerful radar mounted under the nose, and the information it collects is also fed back to the parent ship. In an attack situation, the SH-60B is directed to a suitable launch point, from which it releases its Mark 46 lightweight homing torpedo. It carries two of these torpedoes.

Sensors

The Spruance-class destroyer USS John Young *carries a* ◄ *computer-controlled radar capable of detecting, tracking, and designating specific enemy targets.*

Destroyers need sensors to enable them to detect ships and aircraft as far away as possible, and to classify these as potentially hostile or friendly. If the ships or aircraft are hostile, the destroyers activate the most appropriate weapons system. The warship must be able to detect threat in the air (aircraft or missiles), on the surface, or under the surface. Sensors also enable a destroyer to navigate the oceans and to detect other ships, land, and underwater hazards, such as reefs, rocks, and shallows.

For surface search and navigation, warships use radar, with antennas mounted as high on a mast as possible, in order to give maximum range. Air search and surveillance is also carried out by radar. Older technology required two sets — one for bearing and range, and the second for height — but the latest technology enables all three functions to be carried out by one set, called a "three-dimensional radar." Surface search is also carried out by the traditional means of men using binoculars. Some warships are now being equipped with thermal-imaging

A close-up view of the Mark-23 computer-controlled radar.

equipment, which uses heat signatures to produce a remarkably accurate "picture," which allows an operator not only to detect a target but also to identify it.

Much more complex are the sensors used for ASW. Radar cannot be used underwater, since such high-frequency signals will not travel through sea water. Instead, sonar, which works with sound waves, is used. Sound waves are the one form of electro-magnetic energy that can travel significant distances underwater. There are two forms of sonar, active and passive. Active sonar transmits a sound pulse (typically in the frequency band 7 to 10 kilohertz) that is reflected back by solid objects such as submarines. Passive sonar uses sensitive receivers to detect a submarine's passage through the ocean. Sonars must be located below the surface of the water. On destroyers they are in a large dome at the foot of the bow, in a retractable dome on the ship's bottom, or in a device which is towed behind the ship.

Down below, technicians monitor screens providing information about friend and foe.

In the command information center aboard the USS John Young, crew members study displays on radar-driven consoles.

Destroyer Fleet

The oldest destroyers in service in the U.S. Navy today are eleven ships of the Forrest Sherman and Hull classes. Built in the 1950s, all except one are in reserve; they would only return to service in a time of war. Next oldest, but still all in service with the fleet, are twenty-three ships of the Charles F. Adams class. These have been the standard air-defense destroyers for many years and are employed together with larger missile cruisers to provide air protection for aircraft carrier battle groups. At the time they were built, these were the most powerful destroyers in the world and they remain very effective. In the 1990s, they will be replaced by the Arleigh Burke class, now being built.

The ten Coontz-class ships were completed between 1959 and 1961, and their primary mission is also air defense of battle groups. With 6,510 tons displacement, they are armed with twin launchers for 40 Standard surface-to-air missiles (**SAM**), two quadruple launchers for Harpoon anti-ship missiles, a single 5-inch DP gun, an ASROC launcher, and six torpedo tubes.

The 31 Spruance-class destroyers are the largest class currently in service. These splendid ships joined the fleet between 1975 and 1983 in the biggest single post-war destroyer building program in any navy.

Kidd-class destroyers are designed for general warfare and are the most powerful destroyers in the fleet.

There were 23 Adams-class destroyers built between 1958 and 1963. The USS Waddell was the last.

The Adams-class guided-missile destroyers carry a crew of approximately 360 officers and enlisted men.

They are large ships displacing 8,040 tons, more than double that of the Gearing- and Sumner-class ships they were built to replace. When they entered service in the mid-1970s there was public criticism of the design, mainly because they appeared to be very lightly armed in comparison with Soviet destroyers. This misplaced criticism arose from a misunderstanding of the design philosophies of the two navies. Soviet ships tend to have all their weapons visible on the upper decks, with few, if any, reloads below decks; they also have extensive antenna arrays. U.S. ships, however, have much more sophisticated, multi-role electronic equipment which requires fewer antennas. Similarly, the weapons systems have simple, above-deck launchers and large magazines hidden from view, either in deckhouses or below-deck magazines. Thus, the 5-inch gun and ASROC launcher look lonely on the long, open foredeck of Spruance-class destroyers, but below deck is a vast magazine for the automatic gun as well as 24 reloads for the ASROC launcher. Other weapons include Sea Sparrow SAMs (24 missiles carried), two 20mm Phalanx CIWS, two

USS **Cochrane,** *a typical Adams-class destroyer, is driven by two steam-turbine engines providing a maximum speed of around 30 knots.*

quadruple Harpoon **SSM** launchers, a second 5-inch gun aft, and two triple torpedo tubes. There is a flight deck behind the second stack for two Seasprite LAMPS-I helicopters.

The Spruance class were the first gas turbine-powered U.S. destroyers. The four General Electric LM-2500 gas turbines are based on aircraft engine technology and deliver a total of 80,000 horsepower. Gas turbines have numerous advantages for warships. They are smooth-running, thus causing much less vibration, and are also quiet, making the ship a better ASW platform. A very important advantage, however, is that whereas steam turbines take a long time to work up to full power, a gas-turbine ship can be under way in a matter of seconds and acceleration is very rapid. The

Spruances, for example, can accelerate from a cruising speed of 12 knots to a flank speed of 32 knots in just 53 seconds.

Another virtue of gas-turbine propulsion is that manpower requirements are much less. A Coontz-class destroyer needs a crew of 21 officers and 356 men, whereas the larger, more heavily armed Spruance-class ship needs just 18 officers and 232 men, or a third fewer crew members. This is a very important consideration, since a smaller crew requires less room for accommodations on board the ship, leaving more room for weapons and sensors, or enabling the navy to use a smaller ship altogether. A smaller crew also requires less expense in training officers and sailors.

In their first refits, the Spruance class are being given kevlar armor to protect the most vulnerable parts of the ship, such as the operations center and magazines. At least some of the ships have been fitted with Tomahawk SSM launchers, and others are to be fitted with vertical launch missile tubes in due course.

The U.S. Navy obtained some real bargains in the four destroyers of the Kidd class. In the 1960s and early 1970s, Iran's ruler, the Shah, spent vast sums of money on making the Iranian forces the most modern and powerful in the Middle East. The centerpiece of the naval program was an order for six ships from Ingalls Shipyard, Pascagoula, Mississippi. Called by the Iranians the Kouroush class, these ships were based on the Spruance design but were more heavily armed and had even better sensors. They also had special equipment for hot climate operation, such as dust filters for the air intakes and more powerful air-conditioning.

Ten Coontz-class guided-missile destroyers were built between 1957 and 1959; each vessel displaced 6,150 tons fully loaded.

The USS Benjamin Stoddert *was one of just three Adams-class destroyers to be modernized.*

A navy helicopter approaches the aft deck of the USS Merrill, *a Spruance-class destroyer.*

The order was reduced to four ships, but the Shah was then deposed in a revolution and Ayatollah Khomeini took power. Two months later he canceled the order for these four very expensive ships. The U.S. government then took over the orders at bargain prices, and the ships were completed in 1981 and 1982. They are officially known as the Kidd class, although some navy personnel jokingly refer to them as the Ayatollah class, since without him the U.S. Navy would never have had these ships!

Spruance-class destroyers are basically trimmed-down versions of the design originally proposed for the four Kidd-class destroyers.

USS John Young *under way on a calm sea.*

Arleigh Burke Class

The future mainstay of the U.S. destroyer fleet is the Arleigh Burke class, general-purpose ships capable of carrying out a wide range of assignments in the threat environment of the 1990s and 2000s. The first will join the fleet in 1989 and will be followed by at least 29 more. They will replace the Charles F. Adams and Coontz classes built in the 1950s, but they may also replace Leahy- and Belknap-class cruisers.

Displacing 8,400 tons, Arleigh Burke-class destroyers are built around the Aegis air-defense

The old: Coontz-class guided-missile destroyers were designed more than thirty years ago.

system, which is also used on the Ticonderoga-class cruisers. Aegis has four fixed antenna arrays, rather than the rotating antennas found on earlier radars, and is able to deal with saturation attacks by aircraft and missiles, including sea-skimmers.

Many ships of the 1960s and 1970s incorporated large quantities of aluminum in their superstructure to save top weight, but this has proved to be unwise, since this metal has been discovered to be a fire hazard. As a result, the Arleigh Burke class is of all steel construction. Also, these ships have a very broad hull. This improves their sea-keeping qualities but means that they have less range than previous U.S. destroyers and will need to be refueled more often. They are powered by gas turbine engines, which are 25 percent more powerful than those in the Spruance class.

The new: This artist's concept of the new Arleigh Burke-class guided-missile destroyer hints at the futuristic look all destroyers will have in the next century.

Soviet Destroyers

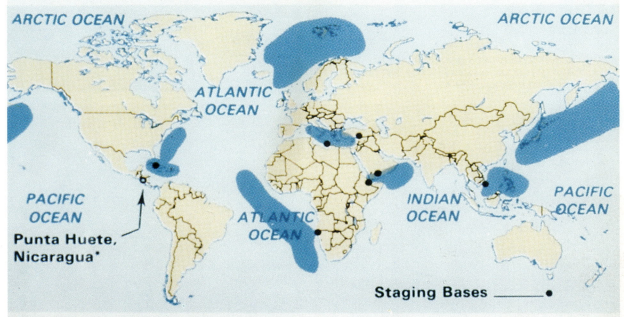

Soviet Naval Reconnaissance Aircraft Operating Areas — 1985

ARCTIC OCEAN

ATLANTIC OCEAN

ARCTIC OCEAN

PACIFIC OCEAN

Punta Huete, Nicaragua*

ATLANTIC OCEAN

INDIAN OCEAN

PACIFIC OCEAN

Staging Bases _____ •

* Newly constructed airfield capable of handling Soviet long-range reconnaissance aircraft.

Soviet naval interests throughout the world are supported by reconnaissance aircraft covering areas where Russian warships currently operate.

The Soviet navy has, at first glance, a large destroyer fleet, consisting of 86 ships. At least 54 of these are twenty years old or even more, however, and their value in a modern conflict would be minimal. Even the Kashin class of 18 ships built in the late 1960s, despite being the first major warships in any navy to be powered by gas turbines, are now out of date, especially in their all-important electronic equipment.

Two more classes are now being built in some numbers, however. These are excellent ships and would certainly give a good account of themselves in any conflict. The Sovremenny class is geared to surface warfare, and the considerable size of these ships (7,900 tons displacement) indicates that they are designed for prolonged voyages in distant waters. The primary surface weapon is **SS-N-**22, with eight

Soviet naval forces include assault transport ships such as the Ivan Rogov. ▶

Soviet naval interests have expanded considerably over the last twenty years and include these vertical takeoff aircraft operated from carriers. ▼

missiles in two groups of four on either side of the bridge; there are no reloads. This missile has a range of 70 **nautical miles**. Next are four 130mm DP automatic guns in two twin turrets, one forward and the second aft. These guns are water-cooled, indicating a high rate of fire, and are mounted in a newly designed turret. Air-defense missile armament consists of two **SA-N-7** launchers, with 40 missiles in below-deck magazines. There are also four 30mm gatling weapons for close-in defense.

One Kamov Ka-27 Helix helicopter is carried. The flight-deck is high, just behind the stack, and there is a new type of telescopic hangar. Surprisingly, instead of being powered by gas turbines, in which the Soviet navy now has considerable experience, the Sovremenny class is powered by a pressure-fired, automated steam propulsion plant, which gives good fuel economy and high acceleration.

These ships, of which six are currently in service, are in many ways the Soviet navy's equivalent to the U.S. Spruance class. There are very few ASW sensors or weapons systems, however, apart from a pair of **RBU**-6000 ASW rocket mounts. These Soviet ships would have to operate in company with ASW ships to ensure their protection against submarines.

Smaller than Udaloy-class destroyers, the Sovremenny-class boats carry one helicopter and several guided-missile launchers.

Soviet Udaloy-class destroyers appeared in 1980 and these powerfully armed ships have facilities for two helicopters.

The second major new Soviet destroyer, the Udaloy class of eight units, is intended to be the ASW escort for a battle group centered upon the Kremlin class of aircraft carriers. ASW armament is exceptionally heavy. There are two quadruple launchers for SS-N-14, one on either side of the bridge, two sets of four torpedo tubes amidships, two RBU-6000 rocket launchers on the superstructure above the tubes, and two Kamov Ka-27 Helix ASW helicopters. Propulsion is by gas turbine. There are four, two on each shaft, giving a total power of 120,000 horsepower. Flank speed is 35 knots and range is 5,000 nautical miles at 20 knots.

Photographs of the Udaloy show a very sharply raked bow. This indicates that there is a large sonar dome below, while the large door at the stern is for a **variable-depth sonar** that is streamed on a cable held on a drum behind the door. There are two single 100mm DP guns, both mounted before the bridge. Air defenses include eight launchers for the SA-N-9 short-range air-defense missile system, with an estimated eight missiles per launcher. There are also four 30mm gatling CIWS.

Soviet naval forces include this Kara-class guided-missile cruiser, one of seven built between 1969 and 1977.

It is interesting that the Soviet navy is producing two separate classes of large and sophisticated destroyers at the same time — one for anti-submarine warfare and the other for anti-aircraft warfare — but is using different hulls and different propulsion systems. Western navies are not allowed to squander resources in this way. In the U.S., Congress keeps close watch over military expenditures. Although the U.S. Navy also uses two classes for these missions, it is a "high/low" mix. The "high" class is Spruance, designed for anti-aircraft warfare. The "low" class is the Oliver Hazard Perry frigate, designed for anti-submarine warfare. This class is much smaller and less expensive than the Spruance.

Other navies, such as the French and Dutch, also have specialized ASW and AAW ships, but they use the same hull and propulsion systems for both classes. Only the armament and sensors are changed to suit the primary mission.

A close-up shot of armaments on the deck of a Soviet warship.

Task Force

The real job of the naval forces is not to wage war but to maintain peace in the sea lanes of the world, which regularly carry trade from country to country.

When we look at modern destroyers, such as the U.S. Navy's Spruance- or Arleigh Burke-class ships, we see vessels covered with weapons systems and sensors. They appear, at least at first sight, to be fully capable of looking after themselves. It would, in fact, be very rare — and probably also very dangerous — for a modern warship to act on its own in today's threat environment. Today the most important role for U.S. destroyers is to serve as elements of surface **task forces**, centered around one or more aircraft carriers or on an Iowa-class battleship.

In such a task force, the main body is formed by the "high value" ships (the aircraft carriers or battleships).

They are surrounded by several rings of protective screens, in which the specialization (anti-surface, anti-aircraft, or anti-submarine) of each unit is fully exploited. Each ship is given a sector to defend, usually about 70 square nautical miles in size, in which it maneuvers continuously. Its purpose is to prevent attacking submarines from gaining the target information they need to fire weapons with a reasonable prospect of success. Due to the maneuvering of the protecting ships and the zig-zag

Destroyers must be flexible, adapt to many naval roles, and operate with speed and efficiency among their larger sister vessels.

course of the main body, the actual speed of advance of the complete group towards its destination is only about 10 knots, but this is the price to be paid for adequate protection.

In the outermost zone and well ahead of the main body are fixed-wing, anti-submarine aircraft, such as the U.S. Navy's land-based Lockheed P-3 Orion or carrier-based SH-3 Viking, or the British Nimrod. These aircraft are equipped with a full range of ASW sensors, including radar, magnetic anomaly detectors (**MAD**), and sonobuoys, all used in combination to detect hostile submarines. Having found a target and identified it as hostile, they can then either deal with it themselves, using their on-board weapons such as torpedoes, depth bombs and rockets, or pass information back to the task force.

The next line of defense for the task force is one or more nuclear-powered attack submarines (**SSN**), which are able to cover a large area of sea. However, such submarines must balance two contradictory characteristics: their high underwater speed (well over 30 knots) enables them to cover large distances

Destroyers work in cooperation with other types of warships to protect convoys.

Battle groups and naval task forces operate in formations that include every type of warship.

U.S. forces frequently operate on exercises with warships from foreign navies.

but creates a great deal of noise. This increases the possibility that they will be detected by the enemy and also makes their own sonar unusable. Their solution is to use a tactic termed "sprint-and-drift," in which they alternately move fast and then lie very quietly in the water, using their passive sonar to detect any hostile ships or submarines.

The next defensive zone is an area patrolled by ASW destroyers and frigates using passive sonar devices. Most effective of these devices are the new "towed arrays." Used by destroyers such as the Spruance and Arleigh Burke classes, the sonar sensors are mounted on a very long cable and towed behind the ship. These arrays are very effective in finding submarines, but they have some drawbacks: to be used to greatest effect, they require the towing ship to move relatively slowly and not to alter course too suddenly. Nevertheless, their advantages far outweigh their disadvantages.

USS Deyo, a Spruance-class destroyer, steams past with ratings on parade.

U.S. naval forces make friendly visits to several countries around the world.

Finally there is the inner screen, in which there are yet more destroyers, frigates, and ASW helicopters. This time, though, they are using their active sonars to detect any hostile submarines that have managed to evade the previous rings of defenses. Many of these ships, and especially the major units, such as carriers or battleships, would also tow noise-making devices, intended to decoy any incoming torpedoes.

Interspersed with these ASW ships will be air-defense ships, providing protection for the task force against enemy aircraft and missiles. These ships are deployed according to a separate air-defense plan. Radar and other electronic devices play the role performed by sonar in the ASW battle, and the weapons are guns and missiles rather than torpedoes and depth bombs.

A task force such as this covers many square miles of sea and consists of many ships, all armed with very capable weapons and fitted with a whole host of effective sensors. Does a submarine even have a chance against this task force? Yes, it does. Even today, finding a submarine is an extremely difficult process because of the nature of the ocean. The layers of water in the ocean behave similarly to (but not identical to) weather in the atmosphere. An ASW ship looking for a submarine can actually pass very close to the submarine but still fail to detect it because the submarine is "hidden" beneath a protecting layer of water. Of course, the ASW ships will find and destroy many of the submarines threatening the task force, but it is the one that they miss that may sink the

Silhouetted against the skyline, an Adams-class destroyer lies at rest on the calm sea.

precious aircraft carrier or battleship. That is why the force moves so carefully, sweeping the ocean as it goes.

Defense of the task force is a very complex task. The threat is three-dimensional, coming from aircraft, surface ships, and submarines. Also, command and control of such a large group of ships, covering a huge area of ocean, is complicated. Incoming information, coming from a variety of sources, must be integrated, interpreted, and then distributed. The commanding admiral's task is both demanding and important. It requires great skill and training, and the decisions a commanding admiral makes can save — or lose — many hundreds of human lives.

Abbreviations

AA	Anti-Aircraft
AD	Air Defense
ASROC	Anti-Submarine Rocket
ASW	Anti-Submarine Warfare
CIWS	Close-In Weapons System
	A multi-barreled gun with a very high rate of fire for "last-ditch" protection, especially against missiles.
DP	Dual Purpose
LAMPS	Light Airborne Multi-Purpose System
	U.S. Navy helicopter-borne ASW system. The two LAMPS helicopters in service are LAMPS-I, the Kamen SH-2F Seasprite, and LAMPS-II, The Sikorsky SH-60B Seahawk.
MAD	Magnetic Anomaly Detector
	A device for detecting submerged submarines.
RBU-	Designation for Soviet Navy ASW mortars. It is always followed by a number, such as RBU-6000, which indicates the range in meters.
SAM	Surface-to-Air Missile
SA-N-	Surface-to-Air — Navy
	U.S. Navy designator for Soviet SAM systems deployed on board warships. Always followed by a type number such as SA-N-4.
SSM	Surface-to-Surface Missile
SS-N-	Surface-to-Surface — Navy
	U.S. Navy designator for Soviet SSM systems deployed on boats and warships. Always followed by a type number, such as SS-N-2.
USS	United States Ship
	Designation for a warship of the United States Navy, such as USS *Bronstein*.

Glossary

Depleted uranium
A non-radioactive form of uranium, of very high density and with a good armor-piercing capability.

Displacement
The measure of the size of a ship, given by the amount of water it displaces. Figures given in this book are for "full-load displacement," when the ship is fully armed, equipped, and loaded for war.

Kiloton
One thousand tons of TNT. Relates to the energy released in a nuclear explosion.

Knot
The measure of speed at sea.
1 knot = 1 nautical mile per hour.

Nautical mile
1 nautical mile = 1.1515 statute miles
= 6,082 feet

Sonar
SOund NAvigation and Ranging. A device using sound waves to detect submerged submarines.

Sonobuoys
Small cylindrical devices used to detect submerged submarines by the noise they emit.

Task force
A tactical grouping of warships, assembled to carry out a particular task.

Variable depth sonar
A device for detecting submarines. A streamlined body containing hydrophones is lowered on a long cable from the fantail of a warship. Its depth is varied to match the underwater conditions.

Index

Page references in *italics* indicate photographs or illustrations.